Buffalo Jones

The Man Who Saved
America's Bison

Carol A. Winn

illustrations by William J. Geer

Rayve Productions

Rayve Productions Inc.
Box 726 Windsor CA 95492

Printed in the United States of America

Library of Congress Cataloging-in-Publication Data

Winn, Carol A., 1957-
    Buffalo Jones: the man who saved America's bison / Carol A. Winn; illustrated by William J. Geer
        p. cm.
    Includes bibliographical references.
    Summary: Recounts the story of Charles Jesse "Buffalo" Jones, a buffalo hunter who undertook a treacherous nineteenth-century Texas trail ride and risked his life to rescue baby buffalo and save their species from extinction.
    ISBN 1-877810-30-4 (alk. paper)

    1. Jones, Charles Jesse, 1844-1919--Juvenile literature. 2. Hunters--West (U.S.)--Biography--Juvenile literature. 3. American bison--Juvenile literature. 4. Wildlife conservation--West (U.S.)--Juvenile literature. [1. Jones, Charles Jesse, 1844-1919. 2. Hunters. 3. Bison. 4. Wildlife conservation.] I. Geer, William J., ill. II. Title.

SK 17.J6 W56 2000
639'.11643'092--dc21
    [B]   99-088345

With love to my husband, Tim, who never gave up on me and never let me give up on myself; to my youngest son, Jonathan, who came home from preschool singing the song that led me to begin this story; to my oldest son, Alex, who was just the right age to listen to this story and give me his suggestions; and to my parents, Buster and June Powell, who introduced me to the joy that I have always found in reading a good story.

—*C.A.W.*

To William and Alma Geer, who tolerated my daydreaming and encouraged me to view the world with passion.

—*W.J.G.*

Acknowledgments

This book would not have been possible without the encouragement and support of the following special people: Ivon Cecil, Beverly Hanlon, Kimberly Willis Holt, Chery Webster, Pat Willis, and Rosalyn Wolfe, members of my critique group, who read multiple versions of my manuscript and made countless helpful suggestions; Lana White, children's literature professor at West Texas A&M University, who helped me focus on the underlying ideology of the story; Robert L. Flynn, novelist and creative writing instructor for West Texas A&M University's summer writing workshop, whose critical eye helped me fine-tune some of the technical details involved in roping a buffalo calf; Joe Ed Coffman, songwriter and musician, whose original song "Buffalo Jones" first inspired me to find out more about this fascinating historical figure; and WenDee LaPlant, Exhibits Curator at Finney County Historical Society, whose assistance in researching the museum's archives was invaluable.

I would also like to offer a special thanks to my editor, Barbara Ray, for her patience with me, her belief in my manuscript, and her vision of the book you now hold in your hands.

—*Carol A. Winn*

Contents

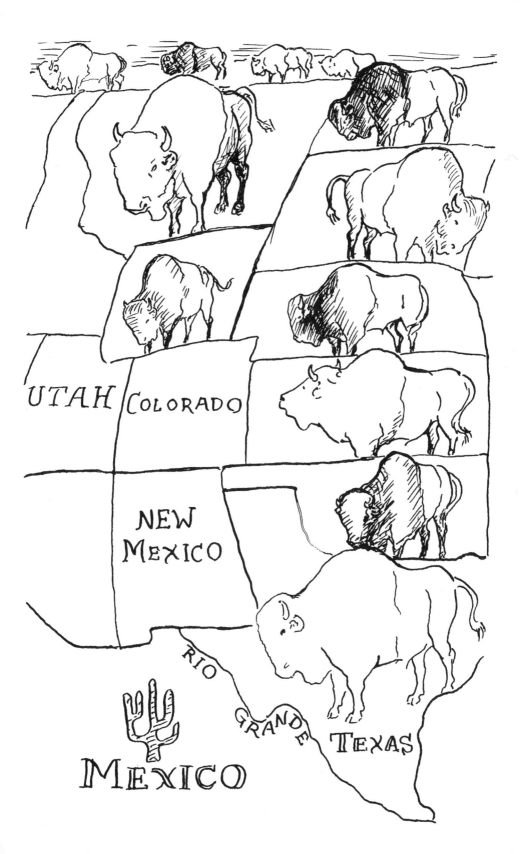

UTAH COLORADO

NEW
MEXICO

RIO GRANDE

TEXAS

MEXICO

Introduction

When Columbus discovered the New World in 1492, it is estimated that more than 60 million buffalo (technically called American bison) ranged from southern Canada through central Texas, a shifting wall of shaggy brown covering the grasslands.

During the 1870s, noisy black steam engines plowed through huge herds of buffalo, stopping only when the sheer mass of the immense creatures kept the train from moving forward. Passengers waited beside the train for up to eight hours while herds crossed the tracks in front of the engine. Impatient travelers shot at the slow-moving buffalo for target practice. Hundreds of animals died beside the tracks, their carcasses left for the wolves, coyotes, and buzzards. Between 1871 and 1873, hunters killed as many as 1,250,000 buffalo each year and sold their hides to leather companies on the East Coast. By 1889, fewer than 600 buffalo remained in the wild.

One man vowed to save the animals he had once hunted. Charles Jesse Jones's lifelong association with buffalo had earned him the nickname "Buffalo Jones." He became known as the Preserver of the American Bison and helped to save the buffalo from extinction. By the turn of the century, he had the largest herd in North America. In fact, Jones's buffalo are the ancestors of many of the more than 25,000 buffalo living today.

When Charles Jesse Jones moved to Kansas from Illinois in 1866, he made his living as a buffalo hunter. He also led hunting expeditions of Easterners who wanted a trophy from the Wild West — a buffalo head to hang on the wall. Jones once said, "Often, in those bloody years, I would promise to break my gun over a wagon wheel when I got back to camp. I am positive it was the wickedness committed in killing so many that impelled me to take measures for perpetuating the race."

Buffalo Jones admired the buffalo for their strength and their ability to survive the harsh conditions on the plains. As he watched their numbers dwindle, he knew he had to act and started his own herd. Unfortunately, he discovered that when adult buffalo were confined, they quit eating and died. Instead of giving up his dream, he brought orphaned buffalo calves to his ranch and used milk cows as surrogate mothers. Most calves raised in captivity grew to adulthood.

Eventually, Buffalo Jones returned to hunting, but instead of shooting adults, he roped buffalo calves. Between 1884 and 1888, he made five expeditions to the Texas Panhandle to capture baby buffalo. Although the hunt of 1886 was one of the most difficult hunts Buffalo Jones ever experienced, he did not run from adversity but faced it head on — like the buffalo he so admired.

Part One: The Storm

It was April 1886. Charles Jesse "Buffalo" Jones sat by the campfire and tugged his pointed white beard as he watched the stars disappear behind swiftly moving clouds. He noticed that the wind had changed directions. It was blowing out of the north now. He frowned when a sudden gust of cold air ruffled the fringe on his leather jacket. "Lord Almighty," he said looking skyward, "not a blue norther." A spell of bad weather could ruin his plans to rescue the buffalo calves.

Jones hadn't expected December weather in April. He knew that springtime snowstorms sometimes blasted the Texas Panhandle, but he figured he'd already missed them. Not that a snow storm would bother the buffalo. The experienced hunter had seen herds of buffalo standing face first into an icy wind, their woolly heads and shoulders covered with snow. He figured that was why they survived. The shaggy part of their bodies kept them warm, even in the worst winter storm.

On the other hand, Buffalo Jones and his horse might not fare so well in a storm. Jones feared they would freeze to death if they rode out to find the buffalo herd in a blinding blizzard.

Besides, when he packed the wagon for the hunt, he hadn't made provisions for a winter storm. He'd brought just enough supplies for six weeks: two weeks to get from Kansas to Texas, one week for the hunt itself, and three weeks to get back home.

Jones planned to capture buffalo calves and lead them back to the milk cows at his ranch. He hoped the condensed milk he'd brought for them would keep them alive on the return trip — if he could get them to drink it. The more calves that survived the 200 mile trek, the better his chance of restoring the mighty buffalo herds to the plains.

The wild buffalo on the Texas plains were the last remnant of the great southern herd that once numbered more than 60 million. Now, there were fewer than 600. Buffalo Jones knew that he had been part of the reason the mighty buffalo herds had almost vanished, and he wanted to be part of their survival. He often thought about breaking his gun against a wagon wheel, but he knew that wouldn't bring back the buffalo he'd already killed. Unless someone found a way to raise and protect some of those that survived, there would be no buffalo left alive by the year 1900. Buffalo Jones had to make sure that didn't happen.

In the distance, a wolf howled, and the horses whinnied nervously. Jones stood abruptly and shook his fist at the darkness beyond the fire. "Stay away from my horses, you varmints!" he shouted. He didn't need wolves scaring Kentuck, his best quarter horse, before tomorrow's hunt.

The wind whipped the fire, and it sputtered. A sudden icy wall of sleet slashed across the campsite. Jones pounded a fist into his other palm. "Sleet," he

groaned, as the frozen rain doused the fire. "That's even worse than snow." He could brush snow off his shoulders before it melted, but sleet would penetrate his clothing and soak him clear through. It was nearly impossible to stay dry during a sleet storm.

Jones lifted the tarpaulin covering the wagon wheels and crawled into the makeshift tent he had made with the help of Charley and Newt. He fell asleep listening to the icy rain slapping the canvas. April storms usually lasted only a day or so. Maybe it will blow over by morning, he thought hopefully.

Instead, the storm's fury increased overnight, and Jones had to postpone the hunt. The great plainsman was restless as he waited for the storm to end. He knew the provisions would not hold out for more than a couple extra days, and then they'd have to start using the stores he had reserved for the trip home. The three men huddled under the wagon with only stale biscuits to eat. They couldn't even light a fire because the buffalo chips they used as fuel were covered with ice. The cold, gray day seemed to last an eternity.

When they woke up the second morning to the sound of sleet still hitting the wagon, Charley and Newt muttered to one another, sneaking occasional glances at Jones. The expedition was not turning out the way Charley and Newt had planned. They hadn't had a decent night's sleep since they'd left Kansas, especially crowded together under the wagon; they were tired of eating cold biscuits; and they were damp from the brims of their hats to the tips of their boots. They were ready to forget about the buffalo and head for their warm, dry beds back in Kansas.

Charley was a schoolteacher and Newt, a farmer. Neither one had even seen a wild buffalo before this. They had come along with Jones to sleep under the open sky and help him capture buffalo calves. Instead, they were sleeping under a leaky wagon and hadn't even caught a glimpse of a single calf. After several minutes, Newt yelled over the howling wind.

"Hey, Buff, don't ya reckon we'd better head on home? Charley and I were noticin' that our supplies are startin' to run low. We were thinkin' . . . "

Jones interrupted, his low voice somehow carrying above the storm. "Thinking we should quit? Go home with an empty wagon and our tails dragging? Thunderation, boys! Why'd you even come with me if you were gonna give up like a couple of cowards?" Jones glared at Charley and Newt. His icy gray eyes bored into them, as if daring them to run away. Charley bowed his head, unable to face Jones's unrelenting stare.

"I reckon you'd best saddle up, then," Jones said calmly, leaning back against the wagon wheel and crossing his arms. His eyes never left the two inexperienced hunters who were huddled together for warmth. "I'm afraid you'll have a long, cold ride."

Newt glanced over at Charley, who looked up and shrugged. Reluctantly, they nodded to one another. Sleeping underneath a wagon wasn't exactly what they'd had in mind, but surely it was better than fighting an ice storm all the way back to Kansas.

"I reckon we're still with you, Buff," Newt said. "We just don't want to starve to death waiting for this storm to end."

"I won't let you starve, boys. As soon as this storm's over, we'll rope those buffalo calves and get them home before they even know they're out of Texas."

Charley and Newt shivered, chewed their tasteless breakfast, and listened to the wind howling outside the tent. They wanted to believe Jones's promise, but an increasing fear of starvation gnawed at their courage.

Part Two: The Chase

On the third morning, the men woke to a different sound. The storm had died down overnight. The wind still whistled shrilly, but the sleet had stopped falling. A cool, gray mist covered the camp, a lingering reminder of the storm, reluctant to release its hold.

Buffalo Jones rose before the sun, his tall frame cramped after being cooped up. He stomped over to the horses and kicked his saddle to knock off the thick layer of ice. He pulled out the saddle blanket he'd been warming under his coat and threw it over Kentuck's back. Next came the saddle, but his frozen fingers fumbled as he tightened the girth. Kentuck shook his head and snorted, ready to begin.

The mules stamped their feet while Newt hitched them to the wagon. Newt and Charley would follow behind Jones, loading the calves into the bed of the wagon along the way.

Buffalo Jones threw his leg across Kentuck's back and called, "I'll leave you a clear trail. Keep an eye out for my calves — they'll be hog-tied. Load 'em up, and take good care of 'em." He looked like a general issuing orders to his troops before a battle.

Newt lifted his hand to the brim of his hat in a halfhearted salute. "Sure thing, Buff." Charley loaded

their remaining supplies into the chuck box, fastened the latch, and nodded as Jones rode away.

The sun rose, bathing the dim landscape in an eerie, reddish glow. Buffalo Jones rode northward, face-first into the biting wind. Spiny mesquite bushes wore a coat of ice that sparkled like thousands of tiny diamonds in the early morning light, but Jones couldn't spare a glance at the beauty around him. Totally focused on the hunt, he watched the frozen ground for signs of the trail.

Kentuck sped across the plain, and they caught up with the herd in less than an hour. Hundreds of shaggy buffalo stretched before him like a wooly brown

blanket, covering the ground as far as Jones could see. He grinned when he saw dozens of calves running beside their mothers. He leaned forward to stroke Kentuck's neck. "Look at 'em, boy. I reckon we'll get a few today." Resting the coiled lasso in his hand, he nudged Kentuck. The horse edged closer to the buffalo.

Suddenly sensing danger, the herd stampeded. A thundering roar deafened Jones as he urged Kentuck on. Jones raced to one side and chose a small, brownish-red calf. He tossed the rope, but the lasso, stiff with ice, wouldn't pull tight. The calf escaped through the open loop.

Determined, Jones tried again. Once more, the rope failed to close around the calf's neck, and the little one leaped to freedom.

The half-frozen cowboy shook the rope, cracking the air like a whip. He shortened the loop and tried again. This time it caught the frightened calf behind the ears. Kentuck stopped abruptly, and the young buffalo fell to the ground, bellowing. Jones grabbed an extra rope from his saddle, jumped down, and tied the calf's hooves together.

Kentuck snorted wildly. Jones's head snapped up, and his eyes swept the plain, straining to see what had alarmed his horse. He spied a gray shadow slinking away, just out of rifle range.

Wolves!

skulking gray shadows.

After sitting in silence for a few minutes, he jumped to his feet and shouted to the distant wolves, "Ha! You're not getting my buffalo!" He pulled off his hat, shoved it between the calf's hooves, and pulled the rope tight. "Wolves won't come near you if you smell like a man," he promised the calf, patting its head. "You'll be safe until Newt and Charley get here." He mounted his horse and galloped after the herd. "That's one," he told Kentuck.

As soon as they caught up with the herd, Jones worked Kentuck between a black calf and its mother. When the little one was far enough from the rest of the herd, he tossed his lariat. This time he caught the baby on the first try. He tied it up and wrapped his coat around its legs to keep the wolves away. "Two," he announced.

When Jones caught the third calf, he twisted out of his vest and buttoned it around the young bison's neck. "Three," he said, smiling. He watched for a moment as the calf struggled, trying to wiggle away from the strange object around its neck.

Jones tugged off one of his boots and bound it to the next calf. As he climbed back into the saddle, he stroked Kentuck's neck. "Keep going, old boy. We're up to four."

Kentuck was tiring from the long gallop, his black coat shining with sweat and steam rising from his flanks. Jones was tired, too. With each toss it was becoming more and more difficult to swing the lasso. All he had on above his trousers were his faded red woollies, so he slapped his arms across his chest for warmth. It was mighty cold with no jacket and no vest, but he wasn't about to quit.

When Jones went after the fifth calf, his rope missed the baby and struck its mother. Startled by the sudden sting, she lunged at him, but Kentuck jumped out of her way. Jones urged him to circle around to the other side of the herd, and they caught up to another calf. Jones had already used all the smaller tie ropes he'd attached to his saddle, so he pulled out his knife and cut a section from his lasso. He felt uneasy, knowing that a shorter catch rope would make it more difficult to

capture a moving animal. It would also be more
dangerous because he'd have to move in closer to the
herd and risk getting knocked off his horse, gored by a
buffalo horn, or trampled underfoot. However, if he
didn't shorten his lasso for this calf, he'd have to stay
put and wait for the wagon. He yanked off his other boot
and tied it between the calf's hooves. "Five," he said.

The icy, metal stirrups stung Jones's stocking
feet. He was glad that the wind had shifted. It was still

cold, but a southwesterly breeze seemed warm compared to the bone-chilling north wind.

Kentuck raced after the herd. By now, the buffalo were exhausted. Their breath puffed into miniature clouds above their heads, and icicles clung to their faces like ghostly beards. Wolves continued to lurk in the shadows, still hoping for a meal.

Jones moved in close, lassoed the sixth calf, and dismounted. With an angry snort, its mother rushed at him. He should have worked it farther away from her before getting off Kentuck, he thought grimly. Jones leaped into the saddle, and the horse lunged away. Since one end of the rope was still tied to the saddle and the other end was tied to the calf, the horse jerked to an abrupt stop. The infuriated mother lowered her horns and charged. Kentuck tried to run, dragging the bawling calf behind him. Soon, they were racing around in a circle with the calf spinning in the center like a wagon caught in a whirlwind.

Jones reached for his knife to cut the calf loose, but the leather sheath on his belt was empty. He must have dropped his knife near the last calf! The frustrated hunter groaned and prepared to meet his maker. The charging buffalo would kill both him and his horse unless he acted quickly.

Part Four: The Danger

With an angry 2,000 pound mother buffalo closing in on him, Jones didn't have time to think. He pulled sharply on the reins and Kentuck stopped abruptly. Then the experienced hunter leaned back in the saddle and pulled out his Winchester. He took a deep breath, aimed, and pulled the trigger.

The buffalo fell, her body thudding to the ground beside Kentuck. Jones sighed and bowed his head. "Sorry, old girl. I'll keep your baby safe for you." A wolf howled nearby, sending chills down Jones's spine. He knew the hungry wolves would devour the dead buffalo cow as soon as he rode away, so he dragged the calf to what he hoped would be a safe distance. When he looked behind him, he saw several ravenous wolves already at the carcass, snarling and snapping at the stragglers who tried to move in for their share.

"Tarnation," Jones muttered. "There's not enough meat for all of them. Once they've polished off the cow, they'll come after my prize. I've got to keep them away from it, but I'm nearly down to nothing." He looked at his legs. "Should I go barefoot or pull off my britches?" The thought of cold iron stirrups on his bare, frozen toes made him cringe, so he sloughed off his pants.

Then, in spite of the intense shivering that overtook him, Jones chuckled. "What a ridiculous

sight we make," he told Kentuck. "Look at me wearing only my red longhandles, wishin' I had my warm trousers on. And then there's that squirming calf lying over there on the ground, kicking up a storm, and trying to get my trousers off his legs."

With a shrug, the cowboy climbed back on Kentuck, still smiling. He didn't have time to linger. With or without his britches, he had to protect his living trophies.

In the time it had taken to capture this calf, the herd had advanced several miles. It took nearly an hour for Kentuck to catch up to it. During the ride, Jones puzzled over what to do next. He'd used the last section of his lasso on the sixth calf. How could he catch a calf without a rope? When the answer came to him, he laughed out loud. He knew exactly what he could do!

When they reached the herd, Jones raced up next to a brownish-black calf, grabbed it by the tail, and jerked it into the air. He jumped off Kentuck and flung the calf to the ground, tying his socks together and wrapping them around its legs. He patted Kentuck's sweaty black nose and proclaimed with satisfaction, "That's seven."

Jones's arms ached from swinging the lariat. His eyes stung from the wind whipping his face. His hands bled where the rope had burned through his calluses, and his bare feet bled where they had frozen to the stirrups. In spite of the pain, Jones felt as if he could ride forever.

Seven calves! Each one meant a better chance to save America's buffalo from extinction. Each would be another step toward his atonement for the crime of slaughtering so many buffalo in his younger days. They would grow up and have calves of their own. Jones pictured hundreds of shaggy brown buffalo covering the hills of his Kansas ranch. These magnificent animals

would once more roam the countryside, and folks like Newt and Charley would no longer have to tag along on hunting expeditions like this one to see wild buffalo.

By the time Jones and Kentuck caught up to the herd, the sunlight was fading. Purple shadows stretched across the plains. The winded calves were too tired to run any farther, and finally the adult buffalo stopped to face the determined plainsman. Jones eyed them carefully as he eased near a calf and reached sideways to grab its tail. Kentuck turned sharply to avoid a mesquite bush and stumbled over the calf, which caused Jones to fly out of the saddle and land in a puddle of slushy mud.

Buffalo Jones stood to wipe the mud off his beard and turned to spit. The calf bellowed hoarsely. Responding to the desperate cry, a group of about twenty adult buffalo immediately broke away from the others and raced toward Jones. With his heart pounding, he vaulted into the saddle. Kentuck twisted and turned, hooves slashing the air, until he broke free from the horde and moved away from the bawling calf. As the calf struggled to its feet, it stopped squalling, and the adults rejoined the herd.

Jones still wanted one more calf, so he rode after the buffalo, shouting wildly. Startled, the herd bolted, and two calves lagged behind. Jones reached for a tail and threw down the larger one. It was strong and managed to get back on its feet. Jones didn't have enough strength left to wrestle it to the ground, so he tripped the calf and held it down with his knees. Shivering violently, he lay quietly on the cold ground and listened to the rumble of the herd as it continued northward.

He also listened anxiously to the snapping and snarling as the wolves crept closer, attracted to the blood on his hands and feet.

Part Five: Going Home

J ones knew it was only a matter of time before the bloodthirsty wolves got brave enough to attack him as he lay on the ground. He stood slowly, lifted the eighth calf to the front of his saddle, and started backtracking.

With the coming of darkness, the wolves grew bolder. When Jones reached the seventh calf, they were already circling, moving in closer to the helpless animal with each round. They backed away, growling, as Jones approached. With aching arms, he heaved the calf up beside the other and dragged himself back into the saddle. Although his fingers were stiff from the day's

activities, he fumbled with the socks he had lashed on the calf's legs. Carefully, he pulled them up over his blistered feet.

"At least this will keep my toes a little warmer," he told his horse. "If I had my boots, old boy, I'd walk beside you. You've got a heavy load to bear." Kentuck walked haltingly back to the sixth calf carrying Jones and two three-month-old buffalo calves on his back. If Jones had waited another month, the calves would have been too big for him to handle by himself.

When they reached the sixth calf, Buffalo Jones made his stand. He flung the two calves onto the ground beside their comrade and drew his revolver. He looked longingly at the fringed leather trousers still wrapped around the kicking legs, but he didn't have time to retrieve his britches. Instead, Jones sat proudly on Kentuck's back wearing only his faded red longhandles and dirty socks, waved his revolver in the air, hollered at the circling predators, and shot at anything that moved. He killed a few wolves and crippled several others. The rest of them cowered and ran away from the noise, but they always came slinking back when Jones stopped shooting and shouting. They sat just out of range, watching him with their hungry, yellow eyes. The weary hunter knew that his supply of ammunition was running low. When it was gone, the starving wolves wouldn't wait long before they moved in to kill him and his buffalo calves.

At last, Jones heard a distant shot and the faint beat of approaching hooves. As the wagon drew near, its creaking wheels and flickering lantern frightened the wolves, who disappeared into the darkness and did not return. Jones could hear them howling as they moved away.

Newt jumped out of the wagon and ran to Jones, holding out a bundle of Jones's wadded up, castoff clothing.

"How many?" Jones croaked.

"Five," said Newt.

"Hallelujah!" Jones shouted hoarsely. "We did it, boys!"

"But Buff, you could've frozen to death before we found you! What were you thinking?" Newt looked at the exhausted plainsman in amazement.

"I was thinking to deprive the wolves of a buffalo dinner," said Jones, grinning as he jammed his crumpled hat onto his head. "I reckon I did just that. These eight calves are growing up in Kansas. Let's go home, boys."

Glossary

bison: A North American buffalo, having a large head and high, humped shoulders. Millions of bison once freely roamed the prairies of central and western United States.

blue norther: A sudden storm producing a rapid drop in temperature and blizzard conditions.

britches: Pants. Trousers. A common name for "breeches," first used around 1880-85.

buffalo: Any of several types of large, wild oxen. An improper though common name for the North American bison.

buffalo chips: Dried buffalo manure, often used to build fires in the Old West.

carcass: The dead body of an animal, especially of a slaughtered animal.

catch rope: Length of rope used to catch animals. Also see **lasso**.

chuck box: A wooden box nailed to the back of a wagon. It has shelves for storing food items and utensils and is closed with a large wooden door hinged on the bottom. When the wagon is stopped, the door is let down to form a cook table.

chuck wagon: A wagon equipped with cooking utensils and food, used as a moveable kitchen, especially on cattle drives and ranches.

condensed milk: Milk with sugar added as a preservative, reduced by evaporation to a thick, syrupy consistency.

gallop: To ride a horse at full speed. In the course of each stride, all four feet are off the ground at once.

girth: A strap around an animal's body that holds a load or saddle securely on its back.

herd: A group of animals feeding and traveling together.

hog-tie: To tie an animal with all four feet together.

lariat: See **lasso**.

lasso: A long rope or line of hide or other material with a running noose at one end, used for roping livestock.

longhandles: Long underwear for men. Also see **union suit**.

mesquite: A type of spiny tree or shrub in west North America, often forming dense thickets.

noose: A loop with a running knot, as in a snare or lasso, that tightens as the rope is pulled.

plains: In the United States and Canada, a vast expanse of flat, mostly dry land east of the Rocky Mountains.

quarter horse: One of a breed of strong horses developed in the United States for short-distance races, usually a quarter of a mile. Their strength and speed make them ideal for ranch work.

saddle: A seat for a rider on the back of a horse.

saddle blanket: A small blanket placed between the saddle and the horse's back.

stampede: The sudden, uncontrolled running of a livestock herd that has been unexpectedly frightened.

Stetson: A felt hat with a broad brim and a high crown, usually associated with cowboys.

stirrup: A loop, ring, or other device, often made of metal, suspended from the saddle of a horse to support the rider's foot.

surrogate: A substitute. A surrogate mother takes the place of the real mother.

tarpaulin: A protective canvas that has been waterproofed with tar, paint, or wax.

Texas Panhandle: A long, narrow, projecting strip of land in northwestern Texas that includes the city of Amarillo.

tie rope: A short length of rope used to tie an animal that has been roped.

trousers: Pants.

union suit: Form fitting, full body underwear for men, usually made of heavyweight cotton or wool for cold weather.

Also see **woollies** and **longhandles**.

varmint: An undesirable or predatory animal.

Winchester: A type of repeating rifle first made in 1866.

woollies: Long winter underwear made of wool.

Also see **union suit** and **longhandles**.

Bibliography

Biggers, Don Hampton. *Buffalo Guns and Barbed Wire.* Lubbock, Texas: Texas Tech University Press, 1991.

Branch, Edward Douglas. *The Hunting of the Buffalo.* New York: D. Appleton and Company, 1929.

Easton, Robert and Mackenzie Brown. *Lord of Beasts: The Biography of Buffalo Jones.* Tucson: University of Arizona Press, 1961.

Easton, Robert and Mackenzie Brown with Gene Caesar. "The Bull Artist Who Saved the Buffalo," *True: The Man's Magazine,* 23-25 & 101-105, September, 1964.

Garretson, Martin S. *The American Bison: The Story of Its Extermination as a Wild Species and Its Restoration Under Federal Protection.* New York: New York Zoological Society, 1938.

Grey, Zane. *The Last of the Plainsmen.* Roslyn, New York: Walter J. Black, Inc., 1936.

Grey, Zane. *Raiders of Spanish Peaks.* New York: Pocket Books, 1966.

Guyer, James S. *Pioneer Life in West Texas.* Brownwood, Texas: 1938.

Hornaday, William Temple. *The Extermination of the American Bison.* Washington: Government Printing Office, 1889.

Inman, Colonel Henry. *Buffalo Jones' Adventures on the Plains.* Lincoln: University of Nebraska Press, 1970.

Inman, Colonel Henry. *The Old Santa Fe Trail: The Story of a Great Highway.* Topeka, Kansas: Crane and Company, 1916.

McHugh, Tom. *The Time of the Buffalo.* Lincoln, Nebraska: A Bison Book, 1979.

Sandoz, Mari. *The Buffalo Hunters: The Story of the Hide Men.* New York: Hastings House, 1954.

photo by Glamour Shots

Carol A. Winn is an award-winning author with numerous published articles in regional and national publications to her credit. She holds degrees from Eastern New Mexico University and West Texas A&M University, and she is a member of the Society of Children's Book Writers and Illustrators and the Panhandle Professional Writers. Ms. Winn, who is also an accomplished orchestral violinist, lives with her husband and two sons in the Texas Panhandle. *Buffalo Jones* is Ms. Winn's first published book.

William J. Geer earned a B.A. in Fine Arts from the Minneapolis School of Art and a Ph.D. in Sociology from the University of Minnesota. He has enjoyed a variety of career successes — as an art director for a publishing firm, creative director for a graphics company, professor and department chair at St. Catherine's College in St. Paul, Minnesota, and owner of a commercial art studio. He currently teaches at Santa Rosa Junior College in Santa Rosa, California, and is a prolific painter and craftsman. He lives with his wife, two stepchildren, two dogs, two cats, and two ducks in northern California.

photo by Chris Peasley

OTHER BOOKS FROM RAYVE PRODUCTIONS

HISTORY

☆ *20 Tales of California: A rare collection of western stories*
by Hector Lee
ISBN 1-877810-62-2, softcover, $9.95, 1998 pub.
Masterfully written stories filled with drama, adventure, intrigue and humor. Mysterious and romantic tales: real life and folklore set in various California locations. They are essentially true, based on historical facts, but folklore abounds, too, as folk remembered the truth or have fashioned it into local legend. Includes ideas for family outings and classroom field trips and discussion questions. (Ages 14-adult)

☆ *Buffalo Jones: The man who saved America's bison* — see Children's Books

☆ *Link Across America: A story of the historic Lincoln Highway* — see Children's Books

CHILDREN'S BOOKS & MUSIC

☆ *Buffalo Jones: The man who saved America's bison*
by Carol A. Winn
ISBN 1-877810-30-4, hardcover, $12.95, 2000 pub.
In this true story, Charles Jesse "Buffalo" Jones undertakes a treacherous 1800s Texas trail ride, risking his life to rescue baby buffalo and save America's bison from extinction. (Ages 10-14)

☆ *Link Across America: A story of the historic Lincoln Highway*
by Mary Elizabeth Anderson
ISBN 1-877810-97-5, hardcover, $14.95, 1997 pub.
It began with a long-ago dream . . . a road that would run clear across America! The dream became reality in 1914 as the Lincoln Highway began to take form, to eventually run from New York City to San Francisco. Venture from past to present experiencing transportation history. Topics include Abraham Lincoln, seedling miles, small towns, auto courts, Burma Shave signs, classic cars and road rallies. Color photos along today's Lincoln Highway remnants, b/w historical photos, map and list of cities along the old Lincoln Highway. (Ages 7-13)

☆ *The Perfect Orange: A tale from Ethiopia*

by Frank P. Araujo, PhD; illustrated by Xiao Jun Li
ISBN 1-877810-94-0, hardcover, $16.95, 1994 pub., Toucan Tales, vol. 2
Inspiring gentle folktale. Breathtaking watercolors dramatize ancient Ethiopia's contrasting pastoral charm and majesty. Story reinforces values of generosity and selflessness over greed and self-centeredness. Glossary of Ethiopian terms and pronunciation key. (**PBS** *Storytime* **Selection**; Recommended by *School Library Journal, Faces, MultiCultural Review, Small Press Magazine, The Five Owls, Wilson Library Bulletin*)

☆ *Nekane, the Lamiña & the Bear: A tale of the Basque Pyrenees*   by Frank P. Araujo, PhD; illustrated by Xiao Jun Li

ISBN 1-877810-01-0, hardcover, $16.95, 1993 pub., Toucan Tales vol. 1
Delightful Basque folktale pits appealing, quick-witted young heroine against mysterious villain. Lively, imaginative narrative, sprinkled with Basque phrases. Vibrant watercolor images. Glossary of Basque terms and pronunciation key. (Ages 6-10) (Recommended by *School Library Journal, Publishers Weekly, Kirkus Reviews, Booklist, Wilson Library Bulletin, The Basque Studies Program Newsletter: Univ. of Nevada, BCCB, The Five Owls*)

☆ *The Laughing River: A folktale for peace*

by Elizabeth Haze Vega; illustrated by Ashley Smith, 1995 pub.
ISBN 1-877810-35-5   hardcover book, $16.95
ISBN 1-877810-36-3   companion musical audiotape, $9.95
ISBN 1-877810-37-1   book & musical audiotape combo, $23.95
Drum kit, $9.95; Book, musical audiotape & drum kit combo, $29.95
Two fanciful African tribes are in conflict until the laughing river bubbles melodiously into their lives, bringing fun, friendship, peace. Lyrical fanciful folktale of conflict resolution. Mesmerizing music. Dancing, singing and drumming instructions. Orff approach. (Recommended by *School Library Journal*)

☆ *When Molly Was in the Hospital: A book for brothers and sisters of hospitalized children*

by Debbie Duncan; illustrated by Nina Ollikainen, MD
ISBN 1-877810-44-4, hardcover, $12.95, 1994 pub.
Anna's little sister, Molly, has been ill and had to have an operation. Anna tells us about the experience from her point of view. Sensitive, insightful, heartwarming story. Excellent for siblings and those who love them. (Ages 3-12) (**Winner of 1995 Benjamin Franklin Award: Best Children's Picture Book**. Recommended by *Children's Book Insider, School Library Journal, Disabilities Resources Monthly*)

☆ *Night Sounds*

by Lois G. Grambling; illustrated by Randall F. Ray
ISBN 1-877810-77-0, hardcover, $12.95
ISBN 1-877810-83-5, softcover, $6.95, 1996 pub.

Perfect bedtime story. Ever so gently, a child's thoughts slip farther and farther away, moving from purring cat at bedside and comical creatures in the yard to distant trains and church bells, and then at last, to sleep. Imaginative, lilting text and daringly unpretentious b/w watercolor illustrations

☆ *Los Sonidos de la Noche*

by Lois G. Grambling; illustrated by Randall F. Ray
(Spanish edition of *Night Sounds*), 1996 pub.
ISBN 1-877810-76-2, hardcover, $12.95
ISBN 1-877810-82-7, softcover, $6.95

☆ *Nicky Jones and the Roaring Rhinos*

by Lois Grambling, illustrated by William J. Geer
ISBN 1-877810-14-2, hardcover, $13.95, 2000 pub.

With the help of four big brothers, Nicky Jones learns to play football, becomes a spectacular player, and surprises teammates and readers in the final scene. This delightful, easy to read story and the lively, colorful illustrations will keep young readers turning pages. (Ages 6-8)

PARENTING

☆ *Joy of Reading: One family's fun-filled guide to reading success*

by Debbie Duncan
ISBN 1-877810-45-2, softcover, $14.95, 1998 pub.

A dynamic author and mother, and an expert on children's literature, shares her family's personal reading success stories. You'll be inspired and entertained by this lighthearted, candid glimpse into one family's daily experiences as they cope with the ups and downs of life. Through it all, there is love, and an abundance of wonderful books to mark the milestones along the way.

"*Joy of Reading* is the perfect guide to great children's books . . . the perfect foundation reference for parents wanting to instill a love of reading and literature in their children. Ideal for developing home-schooling reading curriculums as well."

—*The Midwest Book Review*

COUNSELING

☆ *When a Parent Goes to Jail: A comprehensive guide for counseling children of incarcerated parents*
by Rebecca M. Yaffe and Lonnie F. Hoade
ISBN 1-877810-08-8, hardcover, $49.95, 2000 pub.
Professional counselors help children understand rules, laws, choices and consequences, why their parents are in jail, what to expect in the legal system and how to cope with their emotions. (Ages 5-12)

☆ *When a Parent Goes to Jail Workbook*
by Rebecca M. Yaffe and Lonnie F. Hoade
ISBN 1-877810-11-8, softcover, $29.95, 2000 pub.
This professionally developed companion workbook to the above guide contains writing and drawing activities that help children develop understanding and work through complex emotions. (Ages 5-12)

BUSINESS & CAREER

☆ *Smart Tax Write-offs, 3rd edition: Hundreds of tax deduction ideas for home-based businesses, independent contractors, all entrepreneurs* by Norm Ray, CPA
ISBN 1-877810-08-8, softcover, $13.95, 2000 pub.

☆ *The Independent Medical Transcriptionist, 3rd edition: The comprehensive guidebook for career success in a home-based medical transcription business*
by Donna Avila-Weil, CMT, and Mary Glaccum, CMT
ISBN 1-877810-23-1, hardcover, $34.95, 1998 pub.

☆ *Independent Medical Coding: The comprehensive guidebook for career success as a medical coder*
by Donna Avila-Weil, CMT, and Rhonda Regan, CCS
ISBN 1-877810-17-7, softcover, $34.95, 1999 pub.

☆ *Easy Financials for Your Home-based business*
by Norm Ray, CPA
ISBN 1-877810-92-4, softcover, $19.95, 1992 pub.

ORDER

For mail orders please complete this order form and forward with check, money order or credit card information to Rayve Productions, POB 726, Windsor, CA 95492. If paying with a credit card, you can call us toll-free at 800.852.4890, or fax this completed form to Rayve Productions at 707.838.2220.

You can also order at our Web site at www.spannet.org/rayve.

☐ Please send me the following book(s):

Title _____	Price _____	Qty ___ Amount _____
Title _____	Price _____	Qty ___ Amount _____
Title _____	Price _____	Qty ___ Amount _____
Title _____	Price _____	Qty ___ Amount _____

Subtotal _____

Quantity Discount: 4 items→10%; 7 item→ 15%; 10 items→ 20%

Discount _____

Subtotal _____

Sales Tax: Californians please add 7.5% tax

Sales Tax _____

Shipping & Handling:
Book rate - $3.50 for first book + $.75 each additional
Priority - $4.50 for first book + $1.00 each additional

Shipping _____

Total _____

Name _____ Phone _____

Address _____

City State Zip _____

☐ Check enclosed $_____ Date _____

☐ Charge my VISA/MC/Discover/AMEX $ _____

Credit card # _____ Exp. _____

Signature _____ *Thank you!*